The Phoenix Living Poets

TURNS

Poets Published in
The Phoenix Living Poets Series

★

JAMES AITCHISON

ALEXANDER BAIRD · ALAN BOLD

R. H. BOWDEN · FREDERICK BROADIE

GEORGE MACKAY BROWN · MICHAEL BURN

PHILIP CALLOW · HAYDEN CARRUTH

JOHN COTTON · JENNIFER COUROUCLI

GLORIA EVANS DAVIES

PATRIC DICKINSON

TOM EARLEY · D. J. ENRIGHT

IRENE FEKETE

JOHN FULLER · DAVID GILL

PETER GRUFFYDD

J. C. HALL · MOLLY HOLDEN

JOHN HORDER · P. J. KAVANAGH

RICHARD KELL · LAURIE LEE

LAURENCE LERNER

CHRISTOPHER LEVENSON

EDWARD LOWBURY · NORMAN MacCAIG

ROY McFADDEN

DIANA McLOGHLEN

JAMES MERRILL · RUTH MILLER

LESLIE NORRIS · ROBERT PACK

RODNEY PYBUS · ARNOLD RATTENBURY

ADRIENNE RICH · ANNE SEXTON · JON SILKIN

JON STALLWORTHY

EDWARD STOREY · TERENCE TILLER

SYDNEY TREMAYNE

JON MANCHIP WHITE

TURNS
AND OTHER POEMS

by

RICHARD OUTRAM

CHATTO AND WINDUS

———

THE HOGARTH PRESS

1976

Published by
Chatto and Windus Ltd
with The Hogarth Press Ltd
42 William IV Street
London WC2N 4DF

★

Anson-Cartwright Editions
229 College Street
Toronto, M5T 1R4

ISBN 7011 2151 3

© Richard Outram, 1975

Printed in Great Britain by
Lewis Reprints Ltd.,
The Brown Knight & Truscott Group
London and Tonbridge

STORY

Let us begin with Death
Overheard, in the cry
Of the first breath,

That for what it is worth,
We may all thereby
End with Birth.

Some of these poems have appeared previously under the imprints of The Aliquando Press and The Gauntlet Press.

CONTENTS

CASTAWAY

After the delirium; the thirst;
    the heat like a huge hand;
A landfall at last, with sweet
    water! A realized mirage!
A miraculous atoll, granting
    immediate ease and abundance!

Having been taken by reverent
    natives for God, of course,
And accordingly stripped, anointed,
    garlanded, seated by dignified
Elders in a station of honour
    at the perpetual Ceremonial Feast,

He forgot, well enough, how his tenure
    was subject to chance within time;
How he had until one unaccountable
    error; an eclipse, perhaps, or a tidal
Wave, or a Chief's still-born
    son. They would burn him alive:
Finding nothing irregular in being
    betrayed by their present Divinity;

Lacking His need and reason
    to hold that God is not mad.

RIPARIAN DENIZEN AT HEART

When settled in Eden, I'll dwell by the River;
Where Fire and Water are constantly married,

Remarried, in motion where one may behold
The moment of heavens and oceans in riffles;

But given my present alternative neighbours,
Who would consider living downstream,

To receive the detritus, the flotsam and jetsam
Tangled in sedges or glinting on bottom,

From one who maintains, there is nothing beyond
The Human Imagination; or another

Soul who contends, by night, that beyond
The human imagination, there is Nothing?

AT THE BIJOU

Let the laconic Hero come,
With thirteen shots from his six-gun,
To keep the Maiden from a shame
Far worse than death:
                    within this frame
Ephebe, enthralled, sees Pluto save
Persephone in Plato's cave.

Grotesque figures, vast on the wall,
Are coupling, keeping in common thrall
Sensual creatures watching there,
Coupled in turn: through the darkling air
Behind them, the burdened dove has swerved
Before the bonfire unobserved:
Dropping a broken sprig of light
On her strewn ledge, she takes to flight:
Her kindled shadow is seared upon
The wall both vivid instants, gone
Unseen: she diminishes into the sun,
One nest replenished, one just begun.

Such conversions occur,
Doubtless; in common observation,
Lightning strikes, veining
The distant blackness, a seared
Instant; and holding dying
Brightness in dazzled minds.
Or breaking an ice-white
Bolt in total violence,
Light riven about one!
But after, recovered, one sees
A nearby elm fallen,
Or someone's barn burned.
Lightning strikes; we concede
Annihilations, but invariably
Elsewhere; otherwise, otherness.

How much more comprehensible
Is gradual metamorphosis;
If always marked, granted,
By terrible vulnerable moments
Of alteration; a secret sloughing
Of redundant, translucent skins;
A bitter emergence from waters;
A piercing with fierce light
Of manifold-faceted eyes;
An agonized, timed unfolding
Of unthinkable wings.

SATAN CONSIDERED

Satan Theological

If not omniscient, I can
Assume the consciousness of Man,
Absorbed in elementary games
That creatures may have proper names;
Become that formless, nameless Dread
Which Adam from the Garden fled
In speechless horror, dragging Eve
Still practising her make-believe.

Satan With Musical Box

As long as I have nothing
More pressing, I will wind
This complicated clockwork
With any key I find:

And, when the spring is tightened,
Once more I'll open wide
This drab box which contains you,
With nothing else inside:

Then if a brittle tinkling,
A ragged, plucked refrain
Should set you into motion
And you must dance again,

Why, I will watch intently;
But keeping time until
The mechanism falters
To leave you standing still,

Poised in dreadful balance,
Precarious and free
In naked isolation
For everyone to see:

Then, having altered nothing,
And as you would be hid,
Cowering in your corner,
I'll shut the lid.

Satan Plausible

Remember, symmetrical man,
That should you be severed in twain
I'll join you right back (if I can)
Precisely together again.

And if you are parcelled in four
Quarters and strewn about
I'll find you and patch you up (more
Or less) as you were, beyond doubt.

The problem, for one who is three,
Of how to discover one's Ghost
(According to them, you, or me)
Is but one of a manifold host.

Far better preserve, on the whole,
Yourself which (saving, it's true,
The possible lack of a Soul)
Will, indisputably, do.

Here is the Church;
Here is the steeple;
Open the doors,
See all the people;

Open the people,
See all the lives;
Myriad combs
In myriad hives;

Here is a blade;
Open the combs;
See, in the honey,
Larvae of drones;

Here is a worker;
Given a chance,
See him perform
An intricate dance;

O here is a worm;
See him devour
Comb after comb,
Hour after hour;

See at the core
The cumbent, obscene,
Incessantly bred
Bag of a Queen.

Satan And Chronic Headache

Slow worm-
Gear, worm-
Gear behind the eye-

Ball; lost your bloody marbles,
Random-flashing alleys;
So much for your composure, my Good Man!

My Good Man, skewered on a spit,
Turning on a spit, Sir, driven by a worm-
Gear behind the eye, Sir,

Driven by a worm.

Miner In Hell

Before my single, central eye,
This seam has petered out again;
I'll scrabble to another lie
And scrabble at another vein.

It happened at last,
Beyond my worst dreams.
I will forever suffer
Those choked screams.

Some of us survived.
Beside myself with fear,
I ran till I collapsed
In a limp heap here.

The others may have worked
Their way, I don't doubt,
Through to another shaft.
But I won't get out.

With fetid worm and venomed toad,
The bowels of earth are my abode
Because His curse has been bestowed:
But if I strike the mother-lode

God must relent; as is foretold,
For all His Angels to behold
In adoration, He will mould
Me, in His image, out of gold!

Satan And Magda

(In Hiding)

A single black reed quivers.
The blood-red light decays.
An ant carries carrion
Through an amber maze,

Up over my vast flank.
When the dogs gave tongue
I doubled back through water.
He was not young.

The last day-bird is silent.
As I laid bare my heart
He recoiled in horror.
My lips still part.

Ah, slither closer: cringing,
Reflected in your eye,
Within that diamond darkness
They will pass me by!

(With Dark Veil And Vial Of Vitriol)

I have my role, all
My studied parts;
How dare you call
My vindictive arts

Inhuman? I shall hide
In her bright glass,
Hoping that pride
Brings her to pass

And, fair form, to turn
To her own light:
O God, but I burn
To sear her sight!

(Taunting Satan, Aleatory)

Ah, Lucifer, being only human
    and lacking your ironic command
    of paradox, or your nice

Judgement in matters of moment,
    certain curious virtues continue
    to seem to outweigh vice;

And indeed, Sir, to speak plainly,
    we are hesitant here to entrust
    all to a throw of dice;

An unfortunate aberration, Sir;
    undoubtedly one that you will
    correct, D.V., in a trice.

(Commenting On Her Sister)

A woman wary of extremes,
She entertains sporadic dreams:

In which her naked mother tries
To empty venom from her eyes;

In which her father, grown young,
Extracts the fish-hooks from her tongue;

In which a girl, herself beguiled,
Is suckling a rapacious child;

In which she wears a bloody train
In which to marry Death again.

Poacher

I hear that His Lordship
Has ordered His keepers
To double their efforts.
He values His creatures.

Last evening, they cornered
Old Nick; they beat him
Until he was senseless,
Before they released him.

Well then, he was careless.
He must have forgotten
The first rule of poaching;
Never reveal yourself.

Now, I have a spring lamb,
A plump lamb, for supper;
But fancy young Adam,
Just for the Hell of it.

Knowing his weakness,
Inherent, for likeness,
I'll lure him with mirrors
To bag a vain mortal!

If they should hear his
Squawking and thrashing,
They will not catch me
Cowering in copses;

I shall deceive them,
Having discovered
How to become one
With my given cover;

Thus, while they blunder
Right through me, we'll vanish,
Stealing like lost light
To darkness, to Nothing.

Caliban In Reverie

I have caught an eel;
A writhing treat.
I will peel it to reveal
The oily white meat.

I have stolen onions,
A multitude of spheres;
I will mash them into gruel
Despite my tears.

And I have torn a mare's heart
From her living breast:
A live heart is, of all fare,
By far the best.

You see, I have a captive girl,
All for my very own!
I have crowned her, masked her face,
Placed her on a throne,

Where I will bring my dainties;
Eel, onions, beating heart.
Soon she will come to love me.
Till then we lie apart:

But when she learns to cherish
Me for myself alone,
Then will we cleave together
To the very bone!

For Satan Is Clever

Ah, but no matter
How eager to sever
One from another,

Yet I would never
Hope to discover
When to dismember

Lover from Lover,
Cleaving together
In singular fever

For ever and ever.

OF THE INACCESSIBLE BURDEN OF VISION

The Lion of Lions is stalking the setting Sun;
He is crouched at the livid rim of the red plain:
His Mate has pulled down the Moon before him; she rests,
Guarding her darkening kill until he has slain.

And they shall couple within a complete night;
Covered and covering beast so become entire
That only a bright Covenant parts them at last,
Graced by a single inviolate sphere of Fire.

TWO CATS

Simon

For Simon is sleeping in Egypt:
The Divine Sun bleeds through his closed eyelids.

His flanks rise:
The Sacred River carves deltas strewn with lions.
His flanks fall:
The millet harvest blackens.

He dreams, is forever all momentary fire,
His sky darkens with clamouring waterfowl rising
Out of the emerald swordblade reed beds:

One turned-under paw flexes lightly
On the writhing coils of a garnet-eyed adder.

Igor

Time has cindered him: he is hoar,
Deaf, sometimes palsied: and does adore,
Being translucent, all animate heat:
Stretched heat-sodden, or curled, compleat,
On the carmine hearth let his repose
Hold, if the fire gutters and goes.

A VISION OF THE DEATH OF EROS AND PSYCHE

He is lying folded
In the fetal pose.
She re-enters bearing
A burnt rose.

Together as predicted
On their marriage bed
Singly each discovers
Each is dead.

Side by side, two formal
Figures on a tomb,
They lie speechless, staring
In their room.

In the bitter morning
The cold bolts of the sun,
Manifold, shall pierce them
One by one.

HUNT

We gathered at dawn, stamping
    and slapping our arms in the chill,

Nipping at flasks, coughing
    through the first smoke of the day,

Cursing, impatient, exchanging
    gossip and rumour, arranging

Assignations for after; by noon
    it was over and done with. Although

We rode like devils together,
    took fences, short-cuts, risks

Unthinkable else, yet we came
    dishevelled, splattered, breathless,

Too late to be in on the kill;
    brought to bay near the fountain,

Lame and exhausted, Eros
    was torn to shreds by the pack

Of lies; and we tossed for a trophy,
    a bloody bit of one wing.

ROYAL PHENOMENON

You had me cast without my clothes,
That things might be as they appear;
A monarch naked, head to toes.

I've pigeons nesting in my ear;
An icicle upon my nose;
A slogan daubed across my rear;

No thing of beauty, goodness knows.
Small wonder passing children jeer.
I'm covered only when it snows.

But if the winter is severe,
Deep down within my brazen doze
My old afflictions burn; I fear

That one last time desire chose
To turn the tables: without peer,
My monumental sceptre rose!

Well, well, my subjects may revere,
If not their King, his virile pose.
It never was completely clear,

When I was ardent, why you froze;
Which couldn't matter less, my Dear,
Ars longa somehow, I suppose.

COMMERCE AND TECHNOLOGY

Three perfect billiard balls of premium grade
From one scrivello may be turned, no more;
A firm in London, centre for the trade,
Could reckon thirty thousand in its store.

To bolster profits, minimize all risks;
So homing missiles pierce the last Blue Whales.
Since tourists covet souvenir fly-whisks,
Giraffes are poached just for their tasselled tails.

The charging Rhino falls, four tons of rage;
His horn, as aphrodisiac much prized,
May grant him his extinction in this age.
Like instruments for ours have been devised.

TOURIST STRICKEN AT THE UFFIZI

Dear God, for the rest of my life:
And how shall I tell her, my wife,
That the pallor of a Botticelli Venus
Has come, irrevocably, between us?

BURGHER AND DOXY

'I am anxious to divest myself
   of all superfluous accoutrements,
   both material and spiritual.'

'Cod's-wallop!'

'Further, I am seriously considering
   the practise of ascetic regimens.'

'You'll be sorry.'

'But first, my Sparrow, a little affection,
   a little tenderness, to encourage me.'

'I am here, I am fleeting; catch me
   if you care, if you can.'

ADAM IN THE VERY ACT OF LOVE

But given perfect timing,
Knowledge is all.
I am discovered climbing
The Garden wall;

And if all is distressing
On the other side
Where I have left you guessing,
My sensual Bride,

You shall find on waking,
Beyond doubt,
Just whether I am breaking
In or out.

MERMAID

I

This wave will drag us under,
Fighting tooth and nail;
Oceans cannot quench me!
Sailor, should you fail

To take me for a woman,
Not Mermaid, face to face,
I'll surface in another
Drowned man's embrace.

II

Then they sailed on
Over the fired horizon,
Out of the eye of the storm,

To abandon his body;
This crab-food, this carcass
Sprawled on these rocks.

O he was only a man:
Who hearing my voice,
Despite himself plunged

Into another abyss.
This ocean received him.
I found and embraced him

In fathomless silence
Where we were one
Perishing together.

Now, resuming my song
To break over him,
I must lament unheard

His perilous manhood,
His final ardour:
Never his death.

III

Though I was constantly caressed,
Slow wave on wave,
No infant suckled my salt breast:

And I was wracked with every tide:
And saw your sail
And offered you an ardent bride:

O Mariner, forgive those arts,
That sensual song,
That promised you true woman's parts:

An ocean shuddered as we cleaved:
Hot flesh: cold fish:
A mortal drowned: a Child conceived!

IV

Infant, clinging to my breast,
Blind comfort to your mother
Who perished with one Mariner
To bear, alone, another,

No matter that I suckle you:
Your father's child will never
Rest, by Love constrained, but must
Abandon me forever.

TURNS

Siamese Twins

How shall we say if chance, or fate,
Delivered us coadunate?
Yet much more than a bridge of skin
Conjoins us, each one to his twin:
Examine us and you will find
An unanimity of mind
Unparalleled, save in a brace
Of brothers knitted face to face,
As each invariably bears
The other's agony and shares
In common celebration when
We both are recognized as men
While on display: for we are whole
And pity the divided soul
Who pays his fifty cents to stare,
Forever single, unaware
He is bereaved when he must pass
His twin within a looking-glass.

Tattooed Lady

I loose my robe day after day,
Disdainfully, when I display
My startling charms for those who pay

To watch Saint George, in orange, hack
At purple dragons that attack
Him down the middle of my back;

Then, hors de combat, side by side
And bare as Adam and his bride,
Asquith and Ms. Pankhurst ride,

Surmounted by distinctive flags
Of foreign lands, and azure swags;
Below, an emerald leopard drags

A monkey to a gully where
A roseate and profiled pair
Of striking likenesses must stare,

Each on the other; one is Queen
Victoria in Lincoln green,
The dexter cheek bears Edmund Keane;

Sometimes, for sport, I let them kiss.
Five raggle-taggle tomcats hiss
About my belly; and the bliss

Of Saint Theresa is portrayed
Between two golden sunbursts, rayed
With crimson beams. I am afraid

The Barker seeks to marry me,
Only because he longs to see
My hidden, cherished mystery;

That nest wherefrom blue vipers wind
Out down my thighs: but if I find
A lover, he shall be stone-blind,

That I, as symbol out of sight,
In single naked ardour might
Burn emblazoned through his night!

Wild Man

I'm horrible beyond belief.
A giant Ape befriended
My mother, so the Barker says.
My birth was unattended,

Deep in the jungle's steaming heart.
An infant, I was captured
By native guile; ten Pygmies bore
Me to their Chief, enraptured

With such a prize. He tended me
Until I grew prodigious,
Then sold me to a passing Priest;
Whose motives were religious,

For he discerned a human Soul,
However much perverted,
And sold me into circus life,
A heathen beast converted.

I sit here on my special stool,
Its three legs monumental,
No irons on my ankles now.
I am uncommon gentle.

My penance for my mother's sin
May well, in time, be ended.
The Cross the Father gave to me,
As God, he said, intended,

I fondle constantly: and watch
For one, of all these faces,
To rescue his Immortal Soul
By simply changing places.

Contortionist

Billed as 'THE LIVING PRETZEL',
I can tie my ankles
Into a knot above my head,
A stunt that always rankles

My hosts of jealous rivals;
Let that whole tatty legion
Go, if they are able,
Kiss their lumbar region.

The rubes still come to see,
By watching from all angles,
Sweet something that they shouldn't,
Just covered by my spangles.

My paw, a Gospel-grinder
Who maw, not God, supported,
Would spin to see his daughter
So publicly contorted;

Just think, paw, I was born
Double and triple-jointed,
Thereby for my chosen calling
Divinely appointed.

Dog Act

Dogs, for some reason, cringe
At my slightest reprimand.
Cleo leaps through hoops
Of fire at my command.

Queenie will balance on
One hind leg and bark
Answers to simple questions
From dawn to dark.

Dressed in a tutu, Pearl
Crouches upon the back
Of Hector, who trots around
A tan-bark track.

Peter jumps up and flips
Backwards, to land on his feet.
Solly and Sheba can waltz
Together and keep the beat.

Every night, after the last
Turn, I get dead drunk
Alone in my caravan;
At the foot of my bunk

Bianca, a mongrel bitch
Who is not on the bill,
Lies with her nose in her tail,
Trained to kill.

Bearded Lady

I am in fact a public slave;
How I would love to misbehave
And start the morning with a shave;

But do not dare. Each day I rise
To face my face with downcast eyes
And make the toilette I despise,

So that, my moustache all unfurled,
My whiskers neatly oiled and curled,
I may go forth to face the world.

To bear all day the cruellest whips
Of dirty jokes and jeers and quips;
I am adept at reading lips.

Hell hath indeed, as we are warned,
No fury like a woman scorned:
God knows why I am so adorned.

He may not find, for all His Grace,
A member of the human race
To love me for my hirsute face;

But when the world and time have died
You'll face me, seated by His side,
His radiant and bearded Bride.

The Fattest Man In The World

Great at birth, soon schooled in greed,
Determined early to exceed
And taught prodigious ways to feed,

I gorged myself to Man's estate;
And realized a glutton's fate,
To be this gross incarnate weight.

You, who deride a human hulk,
May sometime learn what visions skulk
Deep in my massive, sluggish bulk:

For I sustain here, while you stare,
Another body in thin air;
And laugh to look below me where

The frozen object of my mirth,
A mottled, Christmas-pudding Earth,
Shrinks in the shadow of my girth;

Where every normal mortal knows,
Who ever laughed at fat man's woes,
The many diabolic throes

I have devised: till I collide,
To share an endless sensual ride,
With one quick, skilful, weightless bride!

Mesmerist

The powers of sleeping suggestion
Are greater than everyone thinks;
I may turn a man to a Goddess;
I have turned a girl to a Sphinx.

I enabled a child to breathe flambeaux
And walk upon embers; so charmed,
He sported like God's Salamander
In rivers of fire unharmed.

I once made a native so rigid,
Three others could rest on his span;
A common enough demonstration:
You wonder just how I began?

I fell out of grace with my father
Who taught me this damnable art
That spoils me for other vocations,
That sets me forever apart,

Thus cursed, to encounter in peril
Somnambulists not as they seem,
Forbidden, however, to save them,
Bereft of the succour of dream;

Compelled, in compassion, to tamper
With ardour, yet never to make
One true transformation: a mentor
My subjects ignore, once awake.

Sword-Swallower

Although in fact
Not possible,
My gullet seems
Bottomless. See
My Adam's apple
Bob. They watch
The act like hawks:
But swallow it.
I engorge swords;
A sabre, a cutlass,
A wicked dagger,
Then pass them all
Round afterwards
To disprove deceit:
Often some poor
Doubting soul
Gets badly slashed.

These razor-sharp
Best Damascus
Blades are real:
But friends, beware,
Always, of evident
Truths. For I
Am insubstantial.

Knife Thrower

My art is to miss exactly.
She waits, her arms akimbo,
Her legs spread, against
The boards, perfectly still.
A luminous skeleton gleams
On the front of her black skin-
Tight costume; she wears
A grinning Death-mask.
Forever, one after another
Like naked flames, I flick
Blades directly at her.
When I stop at last, she leaves
To reveal the precise, glittering
Outline of her body's form.
She was a farmer's love-child;
He would get drunk and beat her
And she begged me to take her away.
Her skin is flawless, she bruises
If you so much as touch her.
She has no choice but to trust me;
At first, she would shut her eyes.
My God, it seems I have come
To love her more than life
Itself, if not than art.

Escape Artist

Ever since my first feat
Proved to be possible,
I practised constantly,
Mastered, in fact, my craft;
I learned to pick handily
Locks of all known makes;
To shatter the strongest links;
To slip the most cunning snare
That one could contrive;
There is no intricate knot
I cannot at last unravel;
They go so far as to say
That there is no box, none,
That can long confine me:

Since she laughed and fashioned,
Loose round my loins,
This delicate circlet,
This simple luminous noose
That I dare not sever,
By God, I am undone!

Funambulist

I work on a slender strand
Slung between two poles
Braced fifteen feet apart.
My patient father coached me
From childhood to fall unhurt,
Then set me again and again
On a crude slack-rope he rigged
Out back of our caravan,
Raising the rope by inches:
Now, I'm the only acrobat
In the world to include in his act,
As finale, a one-hand-stand
Thirty feet from the ground
With no net. I married
A delicate, lithe girl
From another circus family.
We are very happy. She stands
On the circular platform top
Of one pole, to steady me
As I reach the steep, last,
Incredibly difficult slope
Near the pole: when I turn about
To retrace my steps, no matter
How quickly I spin, she is there
At the top of the opposite pole,
Waiting, her arms outstretched.

Midget

In adult stature slighter than
The common children of my kith,
In form I am that giant, Man,
Who once, according to the myth,

From having bested other Gods
Staggered into consciousness,
Thus violating all the odds:
My Lady, let me be, unless,

As I face you, eye to loin,
You might just dare to comprehend
An agony within my groin
And, in humanity, to bend.

Strong Man

Do not deceive yourself, if I seem slight,
Who pinned opponents that no mortal might;

Who tore in two a book so thick, no man
Has ever read it through since time began;

Who drove a trident with a single stroke
Through an impenetrable heart of oak.

Once, over mountains, on my back I bore
Behemoth's weight no man had budged before,

To sink a verdant continent and drown
Its cities where I set that burden down.

Now see my final feat, where I disdain
All common sense and stoop to grasp the chain

Forever round my ankles tightly bound,
To lift myself, at last, up from the ground.